A Child's Day In ...

My Life in
INDIA

Alex Woolf

W
FRANKLIN WATTS
LONDON • SYDNEY

First published in 2015 by Franklin Watts

Copyright © Arcturus Holdings Limited

Franklin Watts
338 Euston Road
London
NW1 3BH

Franklin Watts Australia
Level 17/207 Kent Street, Sydney, NSW 2000

Produced by Arcturus Publishing Limited,
26/27 Bickels Yard, 151–153 Bermondsey Street, London SE1 3HA

Editor: Joe Harris
Designer: Ian Winton

Picture credits:
All photography courtesy of Money Sharma/Demotix/Corbis

A CIP catalogue record for this book is available from the British Library.

Dewey Decimal Classification Number: 954'.0532

ISBN: 978 1 4451 3738 4

Franklin Watts is a division of Hachette Children's Books, an Hachette UK company.
www.hachette.co.uk

Printed in China

SL004299UK

Supplier 03, Date 1014, Print Run 3568

Contents

Morning

Hi! I'm Rajiv. I am twelve years old and I live with my mother, father and sister here in Delhi, India.

Rajiv says ...

Go away, Mum. It's too early. I want to sleep!

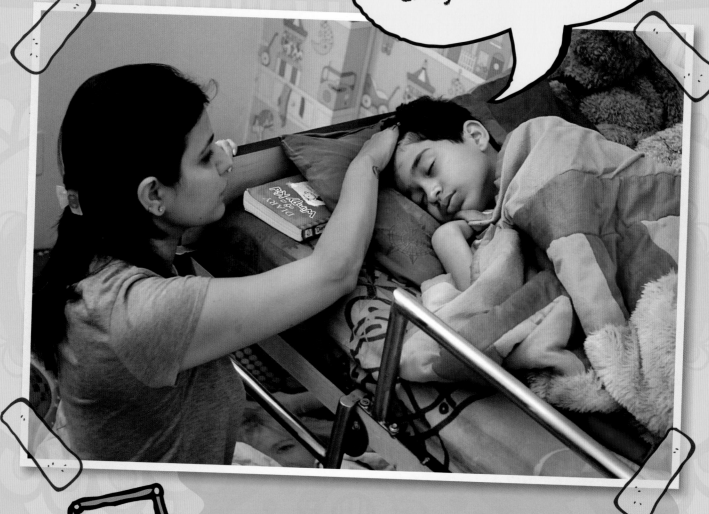

I am woken up at 6.30. After my shower, I get dressed. School uniforms are compulsory in India.

Our school has a typical Indian school uniform: long, dark blue trousers, light-coloured shirt and dark tie.

As I tie my laces on my shoes, I hear Mum calling me for breakfast.

My country

India is an enormous country of 1.2 billion people, located in South Asia. It has a warm climate. Delhi is in northern India.

Getting ready

Mum makes us breakfast. This morning she makes us omelette and chai, which is a spiced tea from India.

Rajiv says ...

I eat breakfast with my sister, Diya.

Diya is nine and goes to the same school as me. We live in a modern apartment in Vasant Kunj, in south-west Delhi. My parents are partners in their own business. They work from home.

I brush my hair and make myself look smart for school.

Mum and Dad wave goodbye as Diya and I set off for school.

Indian breakfasts

We eat a very light breakfast. Traditional breakfasts in northern India could include a *paratha* or *chapati* (types of flatbread) served with vegetable curry, curd and pickles.

Going to school

Diya and I attend Ryan International School, which is also in Vasant Kunj. Diya is in Class IV and I am in Class VII.

Rajiv says...
We take the bus to school each morning.

Our school has over **40** buses ferrying children to and from different parts of the city each day. We must always be polite and listen to the driver.

On the bus I chat with my friend Arjun.

It takes us 20 minutes to get to school. I have my cricket bat with me. Cricket is my passion.

Delhi

Delhi, where I live, is India's biggest city, with a population of 22 million. It contains the city of New Delhi, India's capital.

School assembly

There are many Ryan International Schools in India. They are private schools, so we must pay to be educated here. Most Indian children go to government schools, which are free.

Rajiv says ...
We always start assembly with a prayer.

We are lucky because we go to a modern, well-equipped school. We have a library and computers and excellent facilities for sports, art and music.

We listen carefully to a speech from the principal.

Today, I get a chance to address the whole school. I enjoy public speaking. Of course, I talk about my favourite subject: cricket!

Indian schools

Most children in India attend school. In poorer areas of cities, or in remote areas, there can be up to 60 people in a classroom, and they have very few books.

Lessons

Lessons begin at 8.30. There are 30 pupils in my class. At our school, everyone speaks English.

Rajiv says ...

Today we are learning about the human body.

Our lessons include English, Maths, Hindi, Science, Geography, History and Art.

My friend Arnav and I have made a model to show how teeth are arranged in our mouths.

I am learning Computer Science. We are lucky to have computers - 78% of Indian schools don't have one.

Languages of India

There are over 1,600 languages spoken in India today, and 18 official languages. The most widely spoken language is Hindi, but English is also very common.

Art and music

At ten o'clock, some of us go to the music room, where we are learning to play instruments. I am learning the drums.

Rajiv says ...

I am learning to play rock and pop rhythms.

There are many kinds of music in India. A popular folk style is Bhangra. The unique sound of Indian music is often created by an instrument called a sitar.

We're preparing for a concert at the end of term, which is in June. In India, the school year begins in April and ends in March. We have vacations in June and December.

In our art class, we're making mosaics out of coloured pieces of paper.

Art of India

Our country is famous for its art. Indian artists through the ages have made magnificent bronze sculptures, murals (wall paintings), miniature paintings and jewellery.

Sport

During breaktime, I eat my snack. Mum made me a *paratha* with *dal* (lentil stew) and *raita* (yoghurt sauce).

Rajiv says ...

I chat with my friends about the cricket. I'm happy because India is winning in the test match against England.

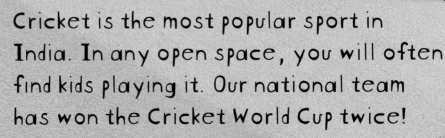

Cricket is the most popular sport in India. In any open space, you will often find kids playing it. Our national team has won the Cricket World Cup twice!

16

I enjoy physical education classes, but sometimes I find it hard to keep in time with everyone else.

I am the opening batsman for my local team. Here I am practising in the nets.

Indian sport

Other popular sports in India include hockey, football, badminton, basketball and *kabaddi*, a type of wrestling.

Hometime

At two o'clock, the bell rings. It's time to go home. Most children take the school bus. A few walk or are picked up by their parents.

Rajiv says ...
Before we leave school we always say our prayers.

Our school follows the Christian faith, but it is open to children of all religions. The majority of schools here are Christian.

Around 82% of people in India are Hindu. But many other religions are also practised, including Islam, Christianity, Sikhism, Buddhism and Jainism.

I chat with Aseem on the school bus. He is a Sikh.

Hinduism

Hinduism is one of the oldest religions in the world. It developed around 5,000 years ago. It is a colourful religion with many rituals. Hindus believe in lots of gods and goddesses.

Lunch

The bus reaches my stop at about half past two. My mother is there waiting for me. Our flat is just a few minutes' walk from here.

Many people in India are vegetarian, meaning they don't eat meat. Hindus believe that the cow is a sacred animal and they never eat beef.

Rajiv says ...

I'm starving, Mum! Is lunch ready?

20

We eat our food on plates, but traditionally Indian food is served on a *thali*, a large, metal platter, with helpings of different dishes served in small metal bowls.

While we eat, Mum asks us about our day.

Indian spices

Spices are essential to Indian cooking, giving flavour to even the simplest dishes. Important spices include cumin, coriander, turmeric, fenugreek, ginger, mustard seed and cardomom.

Out and about

The weather is warm and sunny in the afternoon, and we go out and enjoy ourselves. I practise cricket with my dad.

Our winter lasts from November to February, and our summer from April to June. The monsoon (rainy season) lasts from June to October.

Rajiv says ...

Dad bowls some balls to me in our garage.

Grandpa visits, and he takes us out for a walk.

We stop at a street vendor and Grandpa buys us each an ice cream.

Indian street games

We like to play *chupan chupai* (hide and seek), chain (an 'it' game, where those who are caught join hands to form a lengthening chain) and *kancha* (a game using marbles).

23

Shopping

Later in the afternoon, Mum takes us shopping. Diya wants some crayons and I need a new cricket ball.

Rajiv says ...
Thank you, Mum. This is perfect!

I like the look of this bat, too. But Mum says no. Diya is getting impatient for her crayons.

24

Delhi is a huge international city, and you can buy almost anything here. As well as general stores like this one, there are street markets, shopping malls, arcades and expensive boutiques.

Diya gets her crayons, and Mum buys herself a tube of badminton shuttlecocks.

Indian money

The official currency of India is the rupee, which is divided into **100** *paise*. Rupee comes from the Sanskrit word rupyakam, meaning silver coin.

At home

When we get home from the shops, we do our homework and then play a board game. We watch TV while Mum prepares our supper.

Rajiv says ...

Mum helps me with my English homework.

After we've finished our homework, we play a board game with Dad. The game is called Parcheesi (similar to Ludo) and it's very popular in India.

Dad is very competitive, like me!

Dad and I watch the cricket. Our hero is the batsman Gautam Gambhir, who was born in Delhi.

Indian pastimes

In their spare time, Indians like watching movies (we have a huge film industry based in Mumbai). We play games like Parcheesi, chess and backgammon. Some people enjoy classical dance or yoga. Kite-flying is also very popular.

Evening meal

At half past seven, we sit down for supper. Mum has made us chicken and vegetable curries with *chapatis*, *palak paneer*, *dal*, chopped onion and chutney.

Rajiv says ...
We don't eat with cutlery, but use the chapati to scoop up our food.

Indian food varies from region to region. Northern India is known for *tandoori* cooking. Meat is marinaded in yoghurt and spices before being cooked in a *tandoor* (clay oven).

Bread is popular in northern India, because the land isn't very good for growing rice. *Chapati* is a round flatbread, cooked on a *tava* (hotplate). *Nan*, a puffy bread made with yeast, is cooked in a *tandoor*.

Diya falls asleep quickly, but I'm not very tired so I think I'll read for a while. Goodnight!

Indian sweets

West Bengal in north-east India is famous for its sweets, especially *rasgullas* and *sandesh*. *Rasgullas* are small, spongy balls of curd cheese and sugar. *Sandesh* are similar but flavoured with ingredients like coconut and rose water.

29

Glossary

Bhangra A popular music combining Indian folk traditions with Western pop music.

boutiques Small stores selling fashionable clothes or accessories.

Buddhism A religion founded in north-eastern India in the fifth century BC.

compulsory Required by law or by a rule.

currency The money used in a particular country.

facilities Space or equipment for doing something.

Hindi An official language of India, and the most widely spoken language of northern India.

Hinduism The major religion of India, Bangladesh, Sri Lanka and Nepal. Hindus worship a large number of gods and goddesses.

Islam The religion of Muslims, founded in the seventh century AD by the Prophet Muhammad.

Jainism A religion founded in India in the sixth century BC by the Jina Vardhammana Mahavira.

marinaded (of meat, fish or other food) Soaked in a sauce before cooking to flavour or soften it.

palak paneer A dish consisting of pureed spinach and paneer (farmer's cheese).

paratha An unleavened (made without yeast) flatbread (slightly thicker than a chapati) made with wholewheat flour.

Sanskrit An ancient language of India and the root of many northern Indian languages.

Sikhism A religion founded in Punjab (a region in north-western India) in the 15th century AD by Guru Nanak.

street vendor Someone who sells things in the street, either from a stall or van or with their goods laid out on the pavement.

yoga A Hindu form of exercise and meditation (deep thinking) for health and relaxation.

Further information

Websites

www.bbc.co.uk/news/world-south-asia-12557384
A profile of India from the BBC.

www.facts-about-india.com
A large site containing information about India, its geography, climate, culture, sport and other things.

www.historyforkids.org/learn/india/food/
A website all about Indian food.

www.theschoolrun.com/homework-help/india
Interesting facts, a photo gallery, a list of famous Indians and a quiz.

www.timeforkids.com/destination/india
Facts about India, including a sightseeing guide, history timeline, Hindi phrases and a day in the life of a typical Indian child.

travel.nationalgeographic.com/travel/countries/india-facts/
A guide to India, including fast facts, map, photos and video.

Further reading

India (Been There) by Annabel Savery (Franklin Watts, 2014)

India (My Holiday In) by Jane Bingham (Wayland, 2014)

India (My Country) by Jillian Powell (Franklin Watts, 2013)

India (Unpacked) by Susie Brooks (Wayland, 2013)

India (Countries in Our World) by Darryl Humble (Franklin Watts, 2013)

Index

Series contents

A Child's Day In ...

My Life in BRAZIL

○ Waking up ○ Getting dressed ○ Walking to school ○ Lessons begin ○ Break time ○ Back to work! ○ Lunchtime ○ More lessons ○ School's out ○ Helping at home ○ Downtime ○ Hobbies ○ Dinner and bedtime

My Life in FRANCE

○ My day begins ○ Going to school ○ Registration ○ Morning classes ○ Maths lesson ○ Lunchtime ○ Back to school ○ Afternoon classes ○ Homework ○ Baking a cake ○ Music practice ○ Playtime ○ Dinner and bedtime

My Life in INDIA

○ Morning ○ Getting ready ○ Going to school ○ School assembly ○ Lessons ○ Art and music ○ Sport ○ Hometime ○ Lunch ○ Out and about ○ Shopping ○ At home ○ Evening meal

My Life in INDONESIA

○ Morning ○ Breakfast ○ Walking to school ○ Morning register ○ Lesson time ○ Physical education ○ Playtime and lunch ○ Traditional dancing ○ Hometime ○ Music practice ○ Family shop ○ At home ○ Evening meal

My Life in JAMAICA

○ My home ○ Breakfast ○ Time to go ○ The school bus ○ My school ○ Lessons begin ○ Break time ○ Maths class ○ Lunchtime ○ Afternoon lessons ○ Dance class ○ Shopping ○ Dinner and bedtime

My Life in KENYA

○ Getting up ○ Breakfast ○ Walking to school ○ Lesson time ○ Playtime ○ In the library ○ Eating lunch ○ Afternoon lessons ○ Walking home ○ Fetching water ○ At the market ○ Evening meal ○ Going to bed